Step-by-Step Transformations

Turning Trees into Paper

Dawn James

Cavendish Square

New York

Published in 2015 by Cavendish Square Publishing, LLC
243 5th Avenue, Suite 136, New York, NY 10016

Library of Congress Cataloging-in-Publication Data

James, Dawn, author.
Turning trees into paper / Dawn James.
pages cm. — (Step-by-step transformations)
Includes bibliographical references and index.
ISBN 978-1-62713-007-3 (hardcover) ISBN 978-1-62713-008-0 (paperback) ISBN 978-1-62713-009-7 (ebook)
1. Paper—Juvenile literature. 2. Papermaking—Juvenile literature. 3. Timber—Juvenile literature. I. Title. II. Series: Step-by-step transformations.
TS1105.5.J36 2015
676—dc23

2014002063

Editorial Director: Dean Miller
Editor: Amy Hayes
Copy Editor: Cynthia Roby
Art Director: Jeffrey Talbot
Designer: Joseph Macri
Photo Researcher: J8 Media
Production Manager: Jennifer Ryder-Talbot
Production Editor: David McNamara

Printed in the United States of America

Contents

Paper is made from trees.

5

First, a big **saw** is used to cut the trees down.

The trunks of cut-down trees are called **logs**.

Next, the wood from the logs is cut into very small pieces called woodchips.

Then, water and **chemicals** are added to the woodchips.

This mixture becomes **pulp**.

The wet pulp is put
into **machines.**

13

Next, the pulp is spread out flat.

It lies on a **wire screen**.

After that, another machine
dries the pulp.

Once the pulp dries,
it becomes paper.

The paper is in a big, long sheet.

Finally, a machine cuts the paper into different sizes.

Paper is used for all sorts of things.

We write and draw on paper.

Words to Know

chemicals (KEH–muh–kuhlz) – materials that change one thing into another

logs (LAWGS) – the trunks of trees that are cut down

machines (muh–SHEENZ) – equipment with moving parts that are used to do a job

pulp (PUHLP) – a soft, wet mixture of woodchips, water, and chemicals

saw (SAW) – a sharp metal blade used for cutting wood

wire screen (wy–er SKREEN) – a thin piece of metal with tiny holes

Find Out More

Books

From Tree to Paper
Pam Marshall
Lerner Publications

Paper
Sara Louise Kras
Capstone

Website

How Paper is Made
Idaho Forest Products Commission
www.idahoforests.org/paprmake.htm

Index